Bridget Smith
First Edition published by the De La Warr Pavilion in 2006

De La Warr Pavilion
Marina
Bexhill on Sea
East Sussex
TN40 IDP
UK

www.dlwp.com

Publisher: De La Warr Pavilion Trust Ltd
Editor: Celia Davies

ISBN 0-9541043-6-6

Design SMITH
Printed in Italy by EBS

de la warr
pavilion

Artist's Acknowledgements

My heartfelt thanks to
Celia Davies
Alan Haydon
and all at De La Warr Pavilion
Frith Street Gallery
Michael Dyer Associates
Brian Voce
Stuart Smith
Barney Snow
Shirley Snow
Ann and Peter Smith

Bridget Smith

Bridget Smith

Introduction

UK based artist Bridget Smith was commissioned by the De La Warr Pavilion to respond to its major refurbishment programme between 2003-6.

Smith's photographs capture an extraordinary period in the De La Warr Pavilion's history, a building undergoing a process of transformation and renewal. Taken over a three-year period, a significant body of work by Smith has evolved that transcends a straight-forward documentary approach. Instead, the work intuitively traces a metamorphosis. Smith responds not only to the physical changes, but to the subtle, more ethereal shifts; a sense of contemplation, expectation and a sense of the beyond. The epic architecture of the pavilion gives way to a building seen at once exposed and cocooned; resulting in a photographic reverie of a building changing from the inside, looking out.

The De La Warr Pavilion is a grade one listed modernist building, situated on the South Coast of England. Commissioned in 1935, by the 9th Earl De La Warr it was designed by émigré architects Erich Mendelsohn and Serge Chermayeff. In 2006, following restoration and redevelopment, the De La Warr Pavilion is a major centre for contemporary art in the South East of England. It remains a unique example of outstanding and fully realised modernist architecture in the UK.

This book of photographs demonstrates how this architecturally important building and artistic programme continues to be an impetus for contemporary artists to create new work. My thanks to Celia Davies for nurturing the development of this commission, book and associated exhibition and to Stuart Smith for his deft design of this publication. Finally, we are indebted to Bridget Smith for the unwavering enthusiasm and commitment she has invested in this project.

Alan Haydon, Director

8

10

12

14

16

18

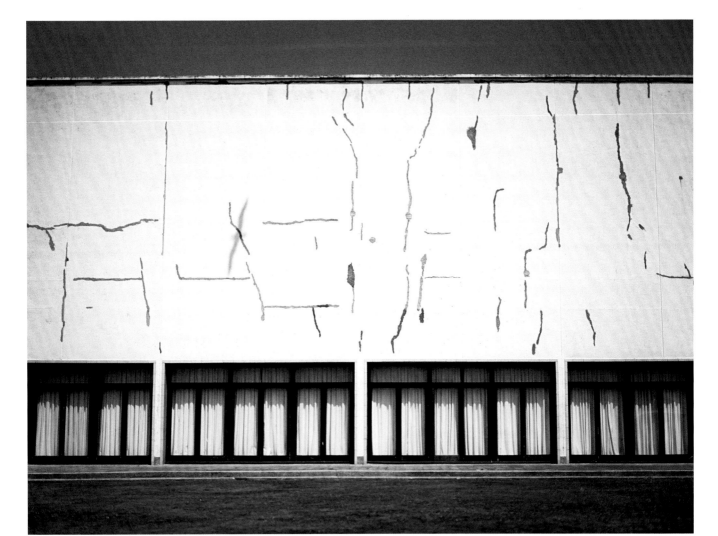

20

22

24

26

28

30

36

40

42

44

46

48

50

52

56

58

60

64

68

70

72

74

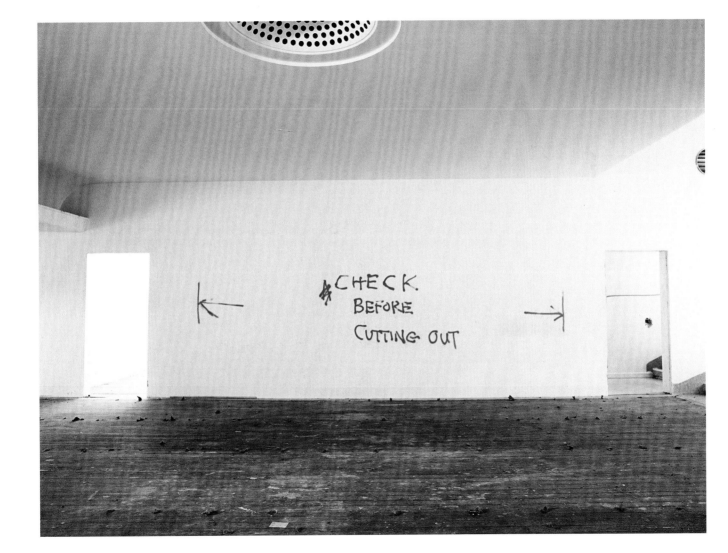

76

78

80

82

84

88

90

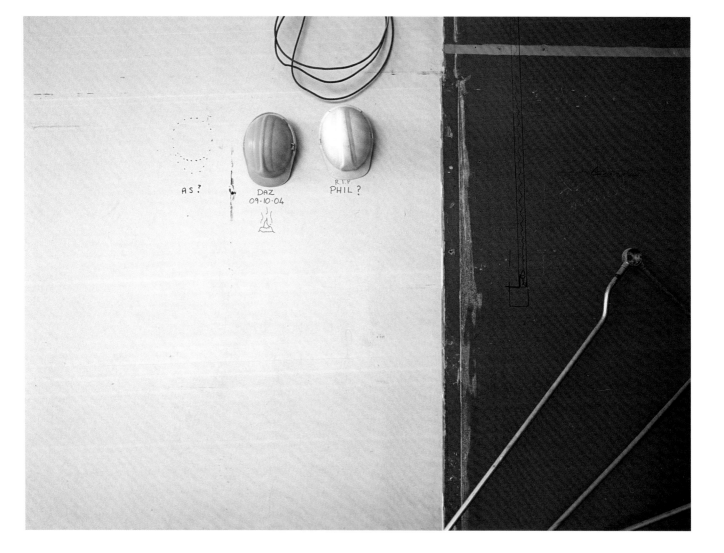

98

100

102

104

108

110

112

114

116

120

122

128

130

134

136

140

142

144

146

148

BRIDGET SMITH

Born 1966 in Essex, England
Lives and works in London.

EDUCATION

1984-85 Central School of Art and Design, London
1985-88 Goldsmiths' College, London
1993-95 Goldsmiths' College, London

SOLO EXHIBITIONS

2006 Rebuild, De La Warr Pavilion, Bexhill on Sea, UK
2005 Cosmos, Frith Street Gallery, London
2003 Galerie Barbara Thumm, Berlin
2002 Salamanca, Centro de Arte, Spain
2001 Gallery Side 2, Tokyo
2000 Frith Street Gallery, London
      Galerie Barbara Thumm, Berlin
1999 British Council Window Gallery, Prague
      Fotogalleriet, Oslo
      Galerie Barbara Thumm, Berlin
1997 Frith Street Gallery, London
      All or Nothing, Studio Gallery, Budapest
1995 Entwistle Gallery, London

GROUP SHOWS

2006 The Expanded Eye, Kunsthaus Zurich
      The Starry Messenger: Visions of the Universe,
      Compton Verney, Warwickshire,UK
      If it didn't exist you'd have to invent it: A partial
      Showroom History, the Showroom, London
      ARCO; presentation of new acquisitions of
      collection Siglo XXI, Madrid
2005 Inner Space, Focal Point Gallery, Southend on Sea
      Our Surroundings, Dundee Contemporary Arts, UK
      Eccentric Spaces, Frith Street Gallery, London
2004 Other Times, Contemporary British Art, City
      Gallery, Prague
      Sodium Dreams, CCS Museum, Bard College,
      New York

Project 1, Elga Wimmer PCC, New York
Faux Real, Borusan Art Centre, Istanbul
Summer Exhibition, Frith Street Gallery, London
Once Again, John Hansard Gallery, Southampton
NEW: Recent Acquisitions of Contemporary
British Art, Scottish National Gallery of Modern
Art, Edinburgh
2001 Give and Take, Jerwood space, London
      ExtraOrdinary: American Places in Recent
      Photography, Madison Art Center, Wisconsin, USA
      Fire Mask God, Galerie Barbara Thumm, Berlin
      Commodity, Firmness and Delight, Globe Gallery,
      Newcastle-upon-Tyne, UK
      Magic Hour, Kunsthaus Graz, Austria
2000 Konfrontace: Czech and British artists in the UK,
      Czech Centre, London
      Because a Fire was in my Head, South London
      Gallery, London
      Real Places, Westfälischer Kunstverein, Münster,
      Germany
1999 Vertigo: The Future of the City, The Old
      Fruitmarket, Glasgow, UK
      0 TO 60 IN 10 YEARS, Frith Street Gallery, London
      Blue Suburban Skies, Photographers' Gallery,
      London
      Natural Dependency, Jerwood Space, London
1998 Inbreeder: Some English Aristocracies, Collective
      Gallery, Edinburgh
      Your Place or Mine, Elga Wimmer Gallery, New York
      New British Photography, Real Gallery, New York
      Made in London (Simmons & Simmons
      Collection), Museu de Electricidade, Lisbon
      Group Show, Frith Street Gallery
      The Tarantino Syndrome, Kunstlerhaus
      Bethanien, Germany
1997 Public Relations, Stadthaus Ulm, Germany
      Within These Walls, Kettles Yard, Cambridge
      History; Works from the MAG Collection, Ferens
      Art Gallery (and tour)

World of Interiors, Binz 39, Zurich
Alpenblick: die zeitgenoessische Kunst und das
Alpine, Kunsthalle Vienna
1996 British Art Show 4, Edinburgh, Cardiff
      Try, Royal College of Art, London
      Ace, Hayward Gallery, London
1995 British Art Show 4, Whitworth Gallery,
      Manchester, UK
      Dorothy Cross, Ceal Floyer, Cornelia Parker, Helen
      Robertson, Bridget Smith,
      Frith Street Gallery, London
1994 The Event, 152c Brick Lane, London
      Close Encounters, Ikon Gallery, Birmingham, UK
      Institute of Cultural Anxiety: Works from the
      Collection, ICA, London
1993 Wonderful Life, Lisson Gallery, London
      Tony Hayward, Jaki Irvine, Ian Pratt, Bridget
      Smith, Riverside, London
1992 Hit and Run, London
      Love at First Sight, Showroom Gallery, London
1991 Rachel Evans, Anya Gallaccio, Bridget Smith
      Clove Gallery, London
      Third Eye Centre, (CCA) Glasgow, UK
      New Contemporaries, ICA, London, (UK tour
      to Hatton Gallery, Newcastle; Hanover Gallery,
      Liverpool)

AWARDS and COMMISSIONS

2003 De La Warr Pavilion
2000 Tate Tokyo Residency
1999 Commission for Vertigo: The Future of the City,
      Glasgow
      Commission for BMW Financial Services
      Commission for Manchester Museum

COLLECTIONS

Arts Council of England
Contemporary Art Society, London
Victoria & Albert Museum, London
BMW
Simmons & Simmons
Government Art Collection
Royal Bank of Scotland
Scottish National Gallery of Modern Art, Edinburgh
Jumex Collection, Mexico City
Denver Art Museum
Cranford Collection, London
Neue Galerie am Landesmuseum Joanneum, Graz

ARTICLES AND REVIEWS

2005   David Barrett, *Art Monthly*, Dec 05/Jan 06
        Martin Coomer, *Time Out*, December
        Jessica Lack, 'Bridget Smith', *The Guardian Guide*, October - November
        Jonathan Jones, 'Eccentric Spaces', *Guardian*, April
        Sarah Kent, 'Eccentric Spaces', *Time Out*, April

2003   Fiona Kearney, 'Book Reviews': 'Bridget Smith, Consorcio Salamanca', *Source*, Issue 36, Autumn 2003, p. 66

2001   'Tokyo Inside Out' Bridget Smith, *Tate Magazine*, Spring 2001, pp. 34 – 37.
        Keith Patrick, 'Sites of Trespass: On the Return of the Narrative', *Contemporary Visual Arts* issue 33, pp. 42-47.

2000   Albert Hill, 'Pretty Vacant', *Blueprint*, Issue 169, February 2000.
        Ossian Ward, 'The Porn Shot', *Limb by Limb*, January February 2000, pp. 42-43.
        Julia Thrift, 'Bridget Smith - Frith Street', *Time Out*, ART - Reviews, February 23-March
        Robert Montgomery, 'Bridget Smith', *Flash Art*, Vol. 33 no 212 May/June 2000 pp. 118.
        Dave Hickey, 'Double or Quits', *Frieze*, Issue 50

February 2000 pp. 62-62.

1998   Robert Mahoney, 'Your Place or Mine', *Time Out New York*, May 21-28 1998, p.59
        Inbreeder: Some English Aristocracies', *Art Monthly*, Issue 217, p. 37
        Susanne Schreiber, 'Eine spannende Ausgrabung und zwei Wiederbegegnungen, Handelsblatt', Gallerien, 12/6/98

1997   Martin Coomer, 'Close Encounters', *Time Out*, May 28-June 4, p.47
        Juan Cruz, Frith Street Gallery exhibition, *Art Monthly*, June 1997, pp.30-32
        John Tozer, 'Within these Walls', *Art Monthly*, September pp. 32-34
        'Within these Walls', *Blueprint*, September 1997, p. 48
        Simon Maurer, 'Sprechende Stilleben', *Tages-Anzeiger, Zürich-Tip*, 24 October 1997
        Review of World of Interiors exhibition: Binz 39, Zürich, 'Kunst' *Annabelle*, 21/97, p.21
        'Kurzkritik - Drei Künstler aus London in der Binz', *Neue Zürcher Zeitung*, 11 November 1997
        'Zürich - Janette Parris, Andreas Rüthi und Bridget Smith in der Stiftung Binz', *Kunstbulletin*, No.11, November 1997
        Mark Durden, 'Hollow Illusions, The Work of Bridget Smith', *Portfolio*, No. 26, Autumn 1997, pp.46-47
        Janice Cheddie, 'I do, I don't', *Womens Art Magazine*, January/February

1995   Sacha Craddock, 'Entwistle', *The Times*, February 14
        Mark Currah, 'Entwistle', *Time Out*, March 8 - 15
        Godfrey Worsdale, 'Entwistle', *Art Monthly*, April
        Ian Hunt, 'Entwistle', *Frieze*, May 1995, pp.59-60
        Martin Maloney, 'Ouverture', *Flash Art*, Summer no.183
        Martin Maloney, 'Glitz and Thrift', *Blueprint*, December 1995

        Adrian Searle, 'British art with attitude', *The Independent*, Section 2, 14 November

1994   David Lillington, 'The Event', *Time Out*, July 13 - 20
        Mark Durden, 'Close Encounters', *Ikon Gallery, Creative Camera*, December-January

1993   Laura Cottingham, 'Wonderful Life', *Lisson Gallery, Frieze*, September - October
        Tania Guha, 'Riverside', *Time Out*, December 29 - January 5

SELECTED CATALOGUES

Bridget Smith, Centro de Arte, Salamanca, 2002.
The Magic Hour, Kuenstlerhaus Graz, Switzerland, 2001.
ExtraOrdinary, American Place in Recent Photography Madison Art Center, USA 2001.
Making Your Dreams Come True, BMW Millennium Project, Hatje Cantz, 2000.
Alpenblick – Die zeitgenössische Kunst und das Alpine, Wolfgang Kos and Kunsthalle Wien ,1998.
Public Relations – New British Photography, Stadthaus Ulm, 1997.
The British Art Show 4, South Bank Centre, London, 1995.

List of Works

C-type prints 34 x 45.5 cm

Courtesy the artist and Frith Street Gallery, London